DRINKING BURGUNDY

Illustration by the Author

The heart of wine. The cross at Romanée-Conti

The 'Drinking for Pleasure' Series

DRINKING BURGUNDY

WRITTEN & WITH ILLUSTRATIONS BY

YOUNGMAN CARTER

HAMISH HAMILTON

LONDON

First published in Great Britain, 1966
by Hamish Hamilton Ltd.
90 Great Russell Street London WC1

Printed in Great Britain by
W. & J. Mackay & Co Ltd, Chatham, Kent

CONTENTS

	page
The History of Burgundy	11
Chablis	22
The Côtes de Nuits	27
Chambolle-Musigny	35
Clos de Vougeot	38
Flagey-Échezeaux	46
Vosne-Romanée	46
Nuits St Georges	50
The Côtes de Beaune	53
The Hospice de Beaune	53
Aloxe-Corton	57
Beaune	60
Pommard	62
Volnay	66
Meursault	68
Puligny and Chassagne	71
Région de Mercurey	75
The Mâconnais	77
Beaujolais	81

Some books on French Wine 85

Some Burgundy Vintages 87

Serving Burgundy 89

A Glossary of Wine Terms in Burgundy 90

Acknowledgements 91

ILLUSTRATIONS

Romanée Conti	*page* 2
Map of Burgundy	10
Burgundian panier	13
Meursault	15
M. Henri de Vilaine	17
Vendange in Burgundy	19
Chablis	24
Dijon	28
Clos de Vougeot	30–31
Clos de Bèze, Chambertin	33
Gevrey Chambertin	36–37
Coopering	40–41
Press at Clos de Vougeot	45
Vendange, Côte de Beaune	47
Nuits St Georges	51
Hotel Dieu, Beaune	54
Gateway to Beaune	56
St Romain, Côtes de Beaune	59
Château La Rôche-Pot	63
The Wine Sales at Beaune	64–65
Château Pommard	67
Volnay	69
Pouligny-Montrachet	72

Moulin à Vent 79
Cuverie in Beaujolais 84
Baccarat glasses 86
Tastevin 88
A Toast to the *Vendange* 92–93

'I closed my eyes and every beautiful thing that I had ever known crowded into my memory.'

MAURICE HEALY
writing of Volnay-Caillerets

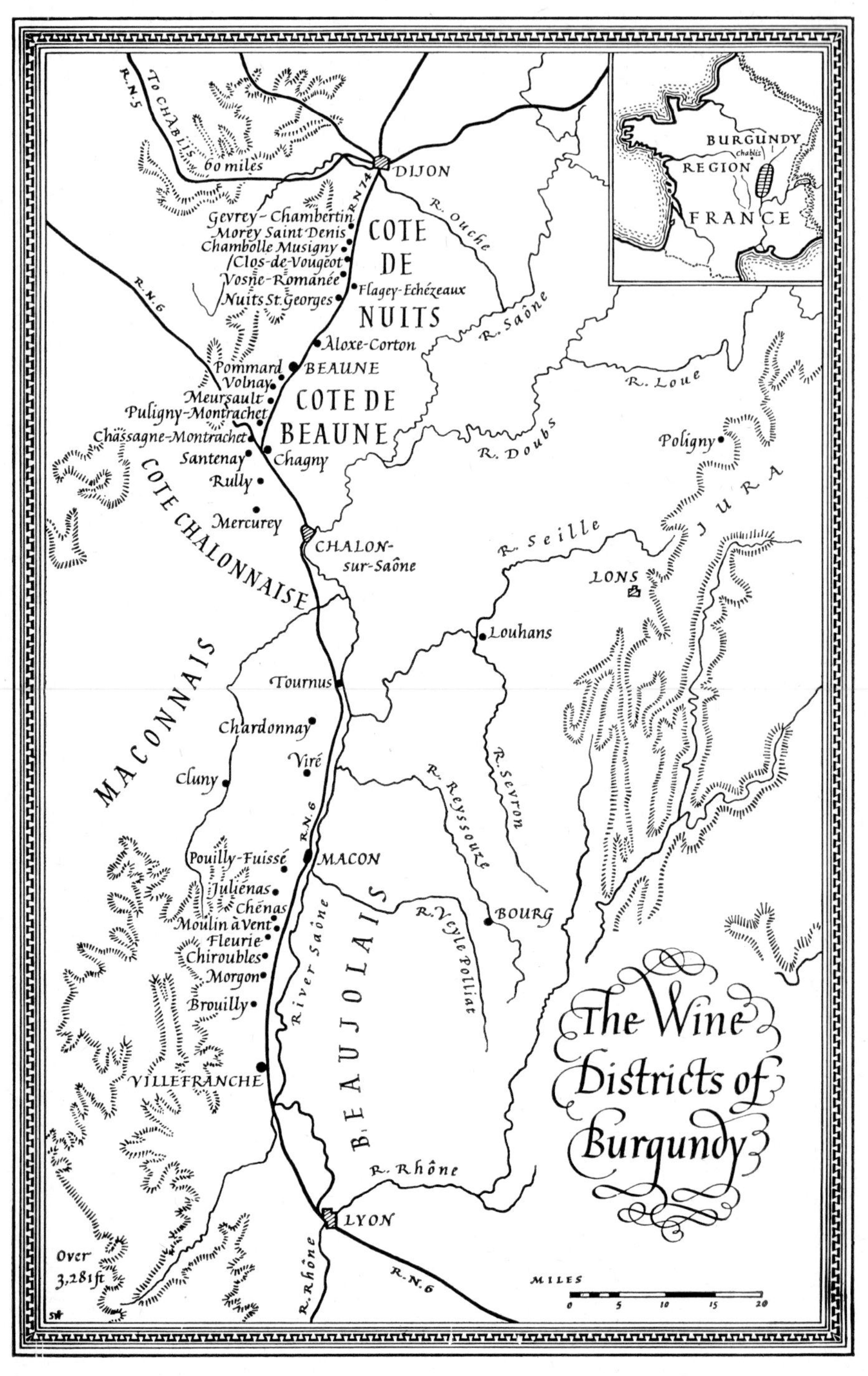

Reproduced by courtesy of Harveys of Bristol

The Arms of Bourgogne

The History of Burgundy

'BURGUNDY at its best overtops Claret at *its* best.' This is the last word on the subject by the greatest of all wine writers, Maurice Healy. He goes on to say that a really great Burgundy is a rare thing, possibly a once-in-a-lifetime experience, but a fine old Claret is not hard to come by if your pocket permits.

Burgundy is so infinitely varied that it cannot be circumscribed by simple definition. To say, for example, 'Claret is the aristocrat, but Burgundy is the all-round good fellow' is only to touch the fringe of a half-truth.

It is a bad generalization to say that red Burgundies are deeper in colour and 'bolder' than Clarets, for certain St Émilions could easily be confused with them if this were the only test. In fact, the vigour of great Burgundies, though it is in their nature, is comparatively recent, for a century ago a percentage of the white Chardonnay grape was used to lighten the wine and to confer the grace and delicacy which was then fashionable. This may have made a more elegant wine, but the natural robust quality of a good burgundy depreciated in the process.

Many Burgundies mature much earlier than Clarets, but they are far shorter lived. Beaujolais may be drunk at a year, Chablis at two, and most of the reds are ready at five, but very few, and of those only the masters, live to thirty years, which is a commonplace with Claret. A shy learner can always, if puzzled, tell a Burgundy from a Claret by the bottle, for the latter is squarer and Burgundy has sloping shoulders. In the matter of quality, a great Burgundy has for me the rolling colourful glory of Beethoven's Emperor Concerto, whereas a Claret of equal stature conjures the magic grace of Mozart or of ballet.

The truth and the choice of simile must rest always with the individual. The new-comer must discover for himself, and this can only be done by comparing a sound wine with its betters and a good minor growth with a great one at its peak. There is no short cut to acquiring a palate.

The variations in Burgundy are as wide as with a collection of paintings of the same school. There may be three masterpieces among them, twenty good works and a rabble of mediocrity which would be very tolerable were it not for the comparison.

History has played the most important role in the creation of this state of affairs, if we allow that the merits of the two great areas are about equal as wine-growing soil. In the Claret country there are great houses, great family names, a tradition of continuous ownership, of squirearchy, and the vital factor that an individual name means an individual product of established quality.

In Burgundy this is not necessarily so; a *commune* or locality here called a '*Finage*' may well possess the advantage of a famous name, for example Volnay. This can be a superb wine, most delicate and supple, but the area is broken up into small holdings with no overall supervision, and as the skill of one small *vigneron* often differs considerably from that of his neighbour, a wine bearing the name to which it is fully entitled may be either superb or indifferent.

The new-comer to the subject must learn to select with caution and, if experience is not to be bought dearly, he must rely upon the good name of the shipper and his wine merchant.

But the key to the understanding of Burgundy lies, as I have said, in its history. No one knows precisely who planted the

The Burgundian panier is the traditional basket used to harvest the grapes

original grapes: some say they grew wild until the tribe called Aedui found their use, some say they came from Tuscany, some from Switzerland, and others that the Phoenicians should take the credit. This theory seems the most probable, for all the great wines of Burgundy lie along the western borders of the old Tin Road, the route by which the Phoenicians brought the metal from the Cornish mines to Marseilles, down the Seine, the Saône, and finally the Rhône to the Mediterranean. But it was undoubtedly the Romans who organized the work on sound farming lines. Caesar does not mention the matter in his commentaries, but he was an austere campaigner and does not refer at all to wine or vineyards. Even so, the Emperor Domitianus in A.D. 89 decided that the local peasants – they were not yet Burgundians – were getting too expert at the job and ordered the vines to be destroyed and replaced by wheat. He seems to have been only partially obeyed, but to have caused a lot of damage all the same, and it was two hundred years before his Act was officially rescinded. The Emperor Probus gets the credit for this.

It was several centuries before the land completely recovered and with the passing of the Romans the rule of order deteriorated. For the first time the land could truly be called Burgundy, for the invading German tribe, the Burgundii, had settled in and colonized the area after their fashion in A.D. 500. But these were uncouth years and wine prospers with civilization. Charlemagne, who united France, restored matters three hundred years later and even introduced some elementary hygiene into the making of wine, for in 809 he forbade his workmen to tread the grapes with bare feet. His own vineyards were at Corton, so it may be taken that he had a benevolent and informed interest in the subject.

The Church was now waxing in power and prosperity and had joined the big landowners, their vines being tended by the religious orders, both monks and nuns, with the aid of lay brethren.

The problem thus raised, even in the Dark Ages, was interesting. The making of wine was profitable, yet its enjoyment was considered sinful by the austere. By a quirk of fate this very austerity led to the establishment of some of the world's best vineyards. Life at Cluny having been considered too luxurious by some of the Benedictines, they broke away and established themselves in a swampy area near Beaune, calling themselves

Some Major Shippers of Burgundy

Lebègue-Bichot
Bouchard Père et Fils
Bouchard Ainé
De Moucheron et Cie
Calout et Cie
Chanson Père et Fils
Chauvenet
Joseph Drouhin
Geisweiller et Fils
Louis Jadot
Louis Latour
Lupe Cholet et Cie
Patriarche Père et Fils
J. Mommessin
Marcilly Frères
Liger-Bellair
Brown Gore & Welch
Pierre Ponnelle
J. Thorin

Guy Gravett

A vineyard at Meursault. *This golden wine has a bouquet said to be like 'ripe peaches with hazelnuts'. Second only to the Montrachet, this is one of the great wines of Burgundy*

Cistercians after the *cisteaux* or bulrush which grew freely on the lower ground. The nuns of St Bernard (himself a prize killjoy), who arrived in 1112, also settled close at hand, where they established what is now the Clos du Tart: the monks created Clos de Vougeot in 1089.

The sparseness of the soil made the growing of other crops difficult and unwise: the pilgrim orders with their motto 'Cross and Plough' were forced into the production of wine if they were not to starve. The Church and the Dukes of Burgundy prospered and grew rich.

The enemy who now appeared was neither war nor pestilence, but a subtler menace. He was, and is, the Gamay grape. Originally brought from the Near East by a Crusader, this interloper produces 50 per cent more juice than the rightful occupant, the Pinot. Unfortunately the quality is inferior, but it is profitable if the produce can be palmed off as good Burgundy. Successive powers and governments have outlawed him through the centuries, but he still flourishes in some areas and has colonized Algeria, Chile, California, South Africa, and Australia, which explains in part why no great wines are yet produced in these countries. He stands as the Jamaican cigar to the true Havana.

From these strictures the Petit Gamay of Beaujolais must be excepted. The Petit Gamay is the upper-class branch of a prolific family, which includes the Gamay Teinturier (the Dyer). It is he who debases the currency.

Philip the Bold, first of the Valois Dukes of Burgundy, son of John the Good, King of France, ordered the destruction of 'this very bad and disloyal plant named Gaamez, from which bad stock comes a great abundance of wine', in 1395, prescribing the pillory for all who disobeyed. He was a wise man. He also had the good sense to ban the storing of wine not grown in the area, knowing that the crafty Burgundians were quite capable of blending their products and palming off the lesser as the greater.

Neither he nor his successors commanded complete obedience: today only the outstanding vineyards are planted with Pinot or the white Chardonnay, and the Gamay is still there plentifully supplying the cheaper products. Only in Beaujolais is he acceptable, for there the soil is not limestone but granite.

Philip the Bold was attempting to grapple with two of the great

Desmond O'Neill

M. Henri de Vilaine. *One of the joint owners of the Domaine of Romanée-Conti, examining a '63 La Tâche by candlelight*

enemies of good wine-making, the use of inferior grapes and the blending of a good wine with a lesser to deceive the buyer. He would have welcomed the *Appellation Contrôlée* of 1935, for he was its original begetter.

This vital piece of legislation makes it an offence to blend two different wines and describe them as originating from a single source, and today the best *vignerons* are among the keenest supporters of the Act. Thus a bottle labelled '*Appellation Contrôlée* – Pommard' must by law contain nothing but wine grown in that district (which is absolutely defined), though it may be a mixture of different vineyards within the area.

There is nothing necessarily inferior in such an amalgam, for the lack of quality in one element may be judiciously supplied by the addition of something more virile from a neighbour's field. But the laws of the boundary are now immutable, though heavy fines are substituted for the pillory if they are broken.

Even so, this is not the way the great wines are produced: these come unadulterated from a few special acres.

The French Revolution, *circa* 1790, did great harm to Burgundy, for it broke up the big estates, sold them off to buyers who resold them in penny packets and destroyed the standards set up over the centuries. Napoleon's praise of Burgundy restored some of the prestige and vastly increased its popularity. Since it could not be shipped directly overseas as at Bordeaux, the wine was handled largely by unscrupulous *negociants*, often collaborating with the *vignerons* themselves, who did not hesitate to dilute good wine with inferior stuff, palming it off as the pure specimen of a great name.

The *Appellation Contrôlée* has put an end, in theory, to this swindle, but in practice it continues, particularly with those Burgundies which ally themselves to inferior Algerian wine and yet preserve a trace of their original character. The *Appellation* stipulates that 10 per cent is the maximum of Gamay grape allowed in some Burgundies and forbids it entirely in others.

There are two methods of protection against these malpractices. The first is to buy only wines carrying the *Appellation Contrôlée* label and the second is to deal with established and trustworthy wine merchants. Beware of labels carrying misleading phrases such as *'Mis en bouteilles dans mes Caves'*, for most wine is bottled in cellars and this of itself means nothing. Again, *'Mis en bouteilles au Château Blank'* has no force in Burgundy, for the wine is not being sold as *'Château Blank'*; it is merely bottled there, and this is no guarantee of origin.

The trustworthy phrases are quite specific: *'Mis en bouteilles au Domaine'*, *'Mis de la Proprieté'*, and the variants on these, all are declarations of fact unless everyone concerned is lying. It is your wine merchant's job to decide for you and not to buy fraudulent goods: his reputation is at stake with every bottle he sells and the best merchants have been in business for a long time.

A greater problem lies in the selection of a wine from a particular and defined area, and this is one of the fundamental differences between Burgundy and Claret. In the Bordeaux area, when the great estates were broken up under the Revolution, syndicates were formed to reunite them so that there could be a true continuity of production, an essential in wine-making. In Burgundy this did not always occur and some of the greatest areas were

Guy Gravett

The *vendange* in Burgundy. *Many of the workers are local but the harvest also attracts students from all over Europe. The pay is usually about 2 N.F. an hour, which works out at thirty shillings a day*

parcelled into lots of a few acres or less apiece. These in their turn were farmed by peasants, often greedy and inexperienced, who did not hesitate to introduce the Gamay grape instead of the Pinot, thereby increasing their quick profit by 50 per cent. Even today many small holders do not own presses, but sell to dealers.

Changes of ownership were frequent, yet the good vineyard continued immediately beside the debased brother, still conferring his reputation on the new false coinage. The well-known social-democratic pattern of levelling down very nearly ruined the reputation of Burgundy. Clos de Vougeot is a case in point. This walled monastic estate of 125 acres 'nationalized' in the Revolution has more than seventy owners, whose holdings range from 5½ acres to a pocket handkerchief. It is not remarkable that there should be considerable variation in quality, even allowing that the slope of the ground favours the upper sections. Yet Clos de Vougeot is fortunate, for to possess a holding here is the greatest status symbol that any Burgundian *vigneron* could imagine.

Thus the reputation of the grower is of vital importance in Burgundy, often taking first place ahead of the name of the wine itself. The shipper, who is sometimes a grower, too, is of equal consequence, for it is he who has to decide which of perhaps a score of different *vignerons*, all producing a wine of one name, is worth exporting.

If, for example, there were a Château Nuits St Georges in the Claret country, then the *negociant* would be purchasing a single product, and his problem would be simply to decide whether or not he wished to deal in it. There is a 'Château de Beaune', but this is an illustrious combine, Bouchard Pere et Fils, with a number of separate holdings throughout the area. It is not a château in the Bordeaux sense of the word. In Burgundy the shipper of Nuits St Georges has to decide between the many small proprietors and risk his reputation on his choice, for the wine is infinitely variable in quality. For the simple wine drinker the shipper becomes the most important figure in the entire proceedings.

The tyro should beware of restaurants who proffer elaborate wine lists without mentioning the shipper. '*Beaune 1959*' has precious little meaning but '*Beaune, De L'Enfant Jésus (Bouchard Père et Fils) 1959*' is a specification of a fine product. No man in his senses if buying a car would consider 'A drop-head coupé 1959' without inquiring if it had been made by Anon & Co. or Rolls-Royce; yet the restaurateur is presenting precisely the same invitation to buy blind.

The exceptions to this rule of thumb occur where an individual vineyard has an identifying name and one proprietor. For example, La Tâche in the *commune* of Vosne-Romanée, one of the great wines of the world, is a single individual masterpiece in its own right and is owned exclusively by M. de Vilaine of the Domaine de la Romanée Conti.

Unfortunately, many of the excellent small vineyards do not enjoy such a wide reputation and the *vignerons* have difficulty in finding a buyer for their output who can afford to preserve its individuality. It is, therefore, sold for blending. Very few of the big merchants are prepared to make a fuss over a small purchase of wine which they may or may not be able to repeat. If by any chance you find such a one and his stock is to your taste, my advice is to look no farther.

At the Revolution the ancient province of Burgundy was divided into four departments which also form the four main divisions of the wine bearing the general name. Yonne to the north, roughly ninety miles from Paris, produces the white wines known as Chablis. The Côte d'Or in the centre starts at Dijon and contains the Côte de Nuits and the Côte de Beaune. Directly south in Saône-et-Loire are the vineyards of Mercurey and the Mâconnais. Beaujolais, at the foot of the group, is in the department of Rhône, but is still a Burgundy.

In describing the wines of Burgundy I have taken the simple wine route starting at Chablis, then crossing to Dijon and moving almost directly south through Beaune to the Beaujolais. It is an ideal tour for the motorist, because good food abounds and the deviations are short, for all the vineyards lie within a few miles of the main road.

I have given the size of vineyards where possible in acres rather than in output, for the reader should be warned that the French are often chary of revealing their yield. Even acreages are sometimes unreliable, particularly in Chablis, for large sections may 'rest' for several years and sometimes a *vignoble* may find itself judiciously incorporated into a more illustrious neighbour. In general I have followed the *Atlas de la France Vinicole*, the official authority, but even this differs from some proprietors.

The Arms of Chablis

Chablis

YONNE has four regions of vineyards: Tonnerre, Auxerre, Avallon and Joigny. They each produce both red and white wines. Of these the most important by far is Auxerre, for it contains Chablis. The wine is dry, very pale yellow in colour, with a touch of green in certain lights. It is fresh and clean, a magnificent quencher of thirst with a suggestion of steel in it which will sharpen the palate for good cooking. The last is the least of its qualities, for the best of the Chablis are worthy of contemplation in their own right. They march excellently with oysters and indeed all shellfish and will also bring out remarkable new flavours in cheese.

They are drinkable early in life, say two years, starting vigorously, if tartly, and keeping up to seven years. The very best, i.e. the most expensive, live longer and darken a little with age.

In 1938 the wines were officially graded as *Grand Cru*, *Premier Cru*, and *Deuxième Cru*, and these titles are used throughout Burgundy. In spite of this and the *Appellation Contrôlée*, only about a quarter, some say only 10 per cent, of the wine described as Chablis or Petit Chablis is genuine, for a large proportion of the wine is sold in cask and bottled by merchants without local responsibilities. It is one of the most popular drinks in France, where ordinary wine is an everyday affair and costly vintages are matters for foreigners and the very rich.

The Grand Crus

Les Vaudésirs Les Clos Les Grenouilles Les Preuses Bougros Les Blanchots	Total of 90 acres

Some Premieres Crus

La Moutonne	Beauroy
Vaulorent	Beugnon
Fourchaume	Châtain
Châpelot	Vaupinent
Montée de Tonnerre	Les Lys
Montmains	Vaillons
Forêts	Pied d'Aloup
Les Butteaux	Séchet
Vosgros	

Note: No acreage figures are available here owing to the proportion of 'resting' vineyards and the tendency of the areas cultivated to decrease.

The reason for the high price of the *Grand Crus* here is not hard to seek. There are only 90 acres of them all, less than one major château in the Médoc, and of these at any time at least half of them may be 'resting', a retirement which takes up to twenty years. Despite the inland mildness of the climate, these are

Peter Waugh

The turrets of the Port Noel, the gate to Chablis

northern latitudes for vines and frost can ravage them as late in the year as May. In 1960 and 1961 most of the crops were destroyed in this way, though what there is of the '61 is considered 'elegant'.

Lack of sun may produce a grape that is too tart to make a good wine, and to combat this sugar is sometimes added to the newly gathered grapes. This is *chaptalisation* and is permitted by law to bring the alcoholic strength up to the authorized figure, 10 to 11 per cent according to the individual wine.

Recently attempts have been made along the route south to disperse threatening hailstorms by the use of 'smudge pots', explosive charges fired into the clouds to break them up, but the science seems to be inexact and no outstanding results are on record.

The *Grand Crus* vineyards, Bougros, Les Preuses, Vaudésir, Grenouille, Valmar, Les Clos, and Blanchots, lie side by side just above the little town beyond the Serein, the stream which runs northwards through the countryside to join the Yonne and finally the Seine. In June 1940 the Italians, for reasons best known to themselves, bombed the centre of the town, and this has now been clumsily rebuilt, but many of the old limestone houses with their dark mossy roofs still survive, as do the twin turrets of the Port Noel, part of the medieval fortifications. All around lies the rolling country of the Grand and Petit-Chablis, classified according to the quality dictated by the favourable nature of the slopes and the soil.

There are 250 acres of First Growths, composed of twenty-four vineyards, in this jigsaw puzzle, and like their betters they sport their names on their labels as a guarantee. To be entitled to the *Appellation Contrôlées* they must use Pinot grapes exclusively and the alcoholic strength must be at least 10·5 per cent.

The rest of the area, makes excellent wine, but there are *vignerons* beyond the limits who are happy to export their products in cask or tanker, which explains in part where some of the so-called Chablis comes from.

The wise drinker, therefore, will buy wine from a specified vineyard and not something with an omnibus label.

Of the lesser vineyards of Lower Burgundy, centring round Chablis, Auxerre to the east, known as La Grande Côte, produces some very acceptable reds, classified as Premières and Deuxièmes. They are highly thought of locally and mature early, but are short-lived. The best of them has the ominous name of Les Migraines, but despite this it has an agreeable bouquet and is a wine of quality. The dry white wines are also deliciously fresh 'on the nose'.

Tonnerre, to the west, makes very respectable fruity reds which are much slower to mature and are a trifle hard or bitter in youth. Les Olivettes is worth noting, along with Les Perrières and Les Pres Hauts. All of them are overshadowed by their neighbours farther south, but they are true Burgundies in their own right.

Avallon, due south, is more famous for its three-rosette Hôtel de la Poste with its fabulous menu, its fabulous prices, and its beautiful garden, than for its wine. Nevertheless both reds and whites are grown there. They are inclined to be rather coarse fellows, high in alcohol and very robust. The Poste itself suggests Chablis and Beaune from a superlative list to match the Écrevisses aux aromates and Poulet en Civet au Vieux Bourgogne, though for my part I prefer a modest wine with high cooking and local products are always worth sampling.

The Chevaliers du Tastevin

The Arms of Dijon

The Côtes de Nuits

Solid, urban old Dijon stands squarely at the head of the Côte d'Or and is its capital city. The long vale south of it is now subdivided into the Côtes de Nuits and the Côtes de Beaune. Curiously, the town is best known for its mustard, which can be bought in every street decked out in 'antique' pots in a variety of flavours, all of them enemies to the palate of a man interested in wine. There is an explanation for this mystery. At Dijon the contents of all casks destined for sale in Paris were given a final examination to see if they were sound. If any had turned to vinegar they were retained, and since a use had to be found for such a liquid it was used for the manufacture of French mustard.

The town has a reasonable hotel, the Cloche, and at least one first-class restaurant, Les Trois Faisans. I suspect that more Cassis than wine is drunk in Dijon, for this slightly alcoholic currant syrup is made here. Mixed with French Vermouth, ice, and soda water it is the great summer apéritif of central France, one of its virtues being that at a café table it can be refreshed from the siphon and spun out indefinitely, or at least as long as

French Government Tourist Office

The Place François Rude in Dijon

the conversation is agreeable. Cassis can also be diluted with white wine and ice and this is commended by experts, though I cannot endorse the claim, as a restorative after a heavy night.

Dijon was the birthplace of St Bernard in 1090, the denouncer of the luckless Abélard and founder of nearly seventy abbeys, including Rievaulx in Yorkshire. He is important to wine drinkers as the formative force of the Cistercians, whose contribution to the vineyards around Beaune he certainly did not foresee.

'If the slopes of the Côte d'Or were not the richest in Burgundy, they would be the poorest', is a well-known local saw, and its truth may be seen all along the road, especially in autumn, when the vines turn to gold above the dull red soil which would be a poor host to any other crop.

The Côtes de Nuits, which start south of the town and are responsible for three-quarters of the finest wine in Burgundy, begin disappointingly with vines which look just like any other, but yield indifferently.

Those nearest the town are relics of the old Côte de Dijon, which had its headquarters at Chenôve, a musty little village on a by-road just out of the town, which boasts the largest ancient wine press in the world. It is indeed a shade more ponderous than those at Clos de Vougeot, but the glory of the phantom Côte has departed, partly on account of the rise of nobler fields farther south and partly because of the sprawling growth of Dijon itself.

It was going strong in the days of Philip the Bold and his wife, the legendary Duchess Marguerite, after whom the great press is still called 'Big Maggie'. She is reputed to have been a lady of the stature of Catherine of Russia, rewarding the lustiest of her *vignerons* very personally for their prowess in the fields and conducting the bacchanalia after the vendange with uninhibited relish.

The wine still made at Chenôve has a black-currant bouquet, but it is otherwise undistinguished. The Clos du Roi is a Gamay wine.

Bishop Gregory of Tours, the great historian who was a profound believer in miracles, writing in A.D. 590, described the Côte de Dijon as 'a rich soil, the hills being thick with vines which provide the inhabitants with a fine Falernian'. This was the highest compliment he could pay, for this was the wine of the Roman Emperors credited by Petronius with living for 100 years.

A mile and a half south of Chenôve lies another little town, Marsannay-la-Côte, a community which has made great efforts to regain its lost prestige by displacing the invading Gamay and restoring the Pinot. Unfortunately, the cost of the original project was not recoverable, for the market for cheaper Burgundies has been lost to Algerian imports.

The vines, however, are now used for the making of a very pleasant rosé, a great deal of which is drunk locally. Nearly all

of what is described by merchants as Burgundian rosé is produced here, and at Couchey, next door.

Despite considerable publicity efforts by the redoubtable *Chevaliers du Tastevin*, of whom more anon, this rosé is not widely known, being overshadowed by those of Provence and Portugal.

As with a great many of the lesser wines of this area the

Guy Gravett

The Château of Clos de Vougeot. *The monastery was built between 1100 and 1551, with many later alterations. It stands at the heart of a walled property of 125 acres. Wine is no longer made in the massive stone* Cuverie *but the house is the property of the Chevaliers du Tastevin who meet regularly to promote the fame of the wines of Burgundy*

production is mostly on the co-operative basis, a word which in France carries no political inference, but means that the small *vignerons*, sometimes holding less than an acre apiece, pool their harvest to produce a wine bearing a common name.

The Côtes de Nuits proper begins at Fixin, a village on a by-road a mile south of Chenôve. It is not a sensational start, most of the wines being more akin to the 'phantom' côte, but the best is Clos de la Perrière, a deep ruby, very vinous, with a reputation for long life, which is classed as a *Premièr Grand Cru*. This one ranks below masters like the Chambertins, but is of their kin, with Clos du Chapitre and Des Hervelets coming a fair second.

On the higher ground behind these there are a great many vineyards many of which produce an *ordinaire* using the Gamay grape. No white wine is grown.

Gevrey-Chambertin is a pleasant enough little town, hardly more than a village, on the great wine road running south to Beaune. Some of its lesser vineyards lie to the east of this line, almost the only ones on the Côte to do so. It was originally called Gevrey and became church property in A.D. 895. Its neighbour, the Abbaye de Bèze, had then been growing grapes for over two hundred years, but the Chambertin vines were not planted until the thirteenth century, when a *vigneron* named Bertin, perceiving how good were the wines of the monastic Clos de Bèze, planted his own field, which lay just next door, with the grape, using the same methods. Hence the Champ de Bertin, or Chambertin as it has remained. They are described locally as 'Little Jesus in velvet pants'.

The two wines at their best are almost identical, full and vigorous, yet graceful with a sort of bold heraldic glory, a distinction born of great breeding.

'There are red Burgundies as good as a good Chambertin,' says André Simon, 'but none better.' And his is the voice of absolute authority.

Napoleon declared Chambertin his favourite wine and carried it all the way to Moscow with him, though he was no connoisseur and had the disgusting habit of watering it. His prestige, coupled with the fact that in this instance he was right, sent the popularity of Chambertin soaring, a fame which has grown with the years.

Guy Gravett

The Clos de Bèze, Chambertin. *Originally a monastic property dating from* A.D. *700 these acres, with their neighbours the 'Champ de Bertin' are some of the richest in the world*

In 1847 the wily *vignerons* of Gevrey, still basking in the glory of this publicity, arranged that the name of the little town should be changed with the aid of a hyphen to Gevrey-Chambertin, the intention being to infer that any local product bearing the name came either from the 32 acres of Chambertin itself or from the 38 acres of Clos de Bèze. But a wine labelled correctly Gevrey-Chambertin may be a very, very ordinary fellow containing no true Chambertin. To add to the difficulty the genuine 70 acres belong to various *vignerons* of differing skill who may harvest their grapes at different times and sell to different dealers.

If, therefore, you are looking for the best, the name of the *vigneron* becomes important, and since it is rarely possible for a new-comer to know such a detail the decision must be taken by the *negociant* or shipper, who, if he is honest, will inform you by the difference in the price he is asking for two bottles of apparently equal merit.

It is important to remember that it is the first name that counts in identifying the rest of the wines classed as Chambertins. For example, Charmes Chambertin, Chapelle Chambertin, and so forth are all individuals of good standing, coming from particular small vineyards, whereas the phrase 'Grand Chambertin' is as meaningless as 'Gevrey-Chambertin'. Maurice Healy calculated that in 1940 in London alone three and a half times as much 'Chambertin' was drunk as could be produced by those historic 70 acres in a twelvemonth and the consumption has been increasing steadily in the last quarter-century. It comes, of course, from the adjoining vineyards of Gevrey, whose owners, or their grandfathers, were astute enough to keep up with the Jones by adding a hyphen.

The Arms of Nuits

Morey is the next village to add to its name. Since 1927 it has been styled Morey-St Denis, to link it with Clos St Denis. The more illustrious properties are the Clos de Tart established by the Cistercian nuns, the Clos des Lambrays, and the Bonnes Mares, which is more than half in the next *commune.* The unlikely name Tart derives from Notre Dame du Tart, near Genlis. Both Clos de Tart and Des Lambrays are absolutely safe wines to buy without disappointment, for they have individual owners with strict standards. They are fine, full-bodied fellows who reach maturity slowly, from five to ten years, and keep well, sometimes up to fifty years, generally improving with age. This is very rare in a Burgundy. It is still, however, considered 'a ladies' wine'.

The Morey-St Denis *commune* or *finage* is a patchwork of small holdings, the best of them lying on the slope of the hills in a continuous belt facing south-east. If only the château system of Bordeaux could unite these divided acres into a group under a single direction, then the resulting elixir could be superb. As these properties are, the wines vary considerably, and this is not due to soil or grape but to the stern individuality of dozens of small holders. Bonne Mares, 'The Good Acres', one of the greatest names, has ten owners with varying ideas, but they are all entitled to the *Appellation* which at its best can rank among the great. Amongst them is the Compte Robert de Voguë, who also owns a large part of Musigny and has Moët et Chandon in Champagne amongst his other properties.

An important and heroic Resistance worker in the war, when he lost two fingers, he is a politician with unlikely ideas for an aristocrat and is probably the most remarkable French vintner of the century.

Chambolle-Musigny

Little Chambolle, hyphenated to Musigny in 1875, lies in a cleft of the hills about a mile and a half from the main road. The name derives from the words 'Champs Bouillant', a reference to the stream running through it which is apt to become a torrent in winter, the hills behind being steep. Chambolle looks across the vale with Les Bonnes Mares, Les Fuées, and Les Cras to its left

The Village of Gevry-Chambertin. *The stone walls which separate one* finage *from the next are characteristic of the whole district*

Guy Gravett

This wine was the favourite of Napoleon who carried it with him to Moscow and thus established its world reputation, though the vineyards are among the oldest

and the Grand and Petits Musigny, Les Charmes, and La Combe d'Orveau just behind the wall of Clos de Vougeot. Between the two Musignys, 25 acres in all, there is nothing to choose: the wine is among the aristocracy. All around is the familiar tight jigsaw of small vineyards, all entitled to the *Appellation* Chambolle-Musigny, all of them of high standing, particularly the Premières Cuvées.

From the Musigny acres themselves a small quantity of white wine is made from the white Chardonnay grape. It is a rarity of quality. Musigny as a vineyard is among the oldest. It was given by Pierre Gros, Canon of St Denis, in 1110, to the fathers of Citeaux and was worked by them and their lay brothers for many centuries, which accounts in part for its excellence, though the estate was broken up before the Revolution. Today there are ten proprietors, among them the redoubtable Compte de Voguë, all of them jealous of the high reputation of their product, which has few peers in all France.

Musigny is a rarely delicate wine and its bouquet has been compared to sweet brier or black-currant. Maurice Healy speaks of 'really good sealing wax' which he meant as flattery: perhaps he patronized a very special stationer. But it is a wine of infinite finesse, less gloriously baroque than some of its neighbours just to the south, a nobleman in its own right. Do not, I beg of you, find yourself put off by these highfalutin' phrases: good things of this sort do not readily translate into words. Try the wine and compose your own eulogies.

Bonnes Mares is of the same school, perhaps a little less elegant, but caressing to the palate and as subtly pleasing as a witty whisper. On this plane of eminence who can judge between bottle and bottle? We are in the company of the masters here and must pay our respects with gratitude.

Clos de Vougeot

VOUGEOT, as a name, is the odd man out among the villages of the Côte, for it was originally Gilly-les-Vougeot and has dropped the prefix. Probably this is because the 125 acres of Clos de Vougeot, surrounded by a monastic wall of split stone, is the only vineyard of importance. It is named after the Vouge stream. The huge

Gevrey-Chambertin

Têtes de Cuvées (also called Crus Hors Ligne)

	acres
Le Chambertin	32·5
Le Chambertin Clos de Bèze	37·5

Premières Cuvées

Chapelle-Chambertin	13
Charmes-Chambertin	31
Griottes-Chambertin	13·5
Latricières-Chambertin	31·5
Mazys-Chambertin	31·5
Mazoyères-Chambertin	47·5
Ruchottes-Chambertin	8·5
Cazatiers	20
Clos St Jacques	17·5
Étournelles	5
Fouchère	2·5
Les Varoilles	15
Les Griottes	13·5
Les Latricières	17·5

Morey-St Denis

Têtes de Cuvées

	acres
Bonnes Mares (part)	5
Clos de Tart	17·5
Clos des Lambrays	22

Premières Cuvées

Clos St Denis	116
Clos de la Roche	138
Les Charnières	6
Les Chenevery	8
Aux Cheseaux	6
Clos des Ormes	11
Les Faconnières	4·5
Les Millandes	11
Monts-Luisants (white wine)	8
Morey	8
Clos Sorbet	8

Photos: Guy Gravett

The Tonneliers. *Coopering at St Romain in the Hautes Côtes de Beaune. This ancient craft is the indispensable twin to the vintners skill. 'The Wine and the Wood' is one of the time honoured toasts at all vintners gatherings. For many of the best wines only new casks of oak are used and for maturing wine no substitute has ever been discovered. Before fitting the lower hoop the cooper winches in the stave ends with a wire tackle and then persuades the staves to set by wetting the outside of the cask and heating the inside. The craft of the 'Tonneliers' is generally hereditary*

Chambolle-Musigny

Têtes de Cuvées

	acres
Les Musigny	25
Les Bonne Mares	34

Premières Cuvées

Les Amoureuses	13·5
Les Baudes	9
Les Charmes	14·5
La Combe d'Orveau	12·5
Les Cras	10·5
Les Fuèes	15·5
Les Gruenchers	7·5
Les Noirots	7·5
Les Sentiers	12·5

Clos de Vougeot

Some Major Owners:

	acres
André, P.	2·6
Arnoux, Charles	1
Champy, Père et Fils	5·2
Clair-Daü	1
Drouhin, J.	2·3
Drouhin-Laroze	1·6
Engel, René	3
Faively, J.	2
Gouroux Frères	2·2
Grivelet-Cusset	1·5
Grivot, G.	4·5
Gros, Louis	5·6
Jaboulet-Vercherre	1·5
Jaffelin	1·5
Lejay-Lagoutte	4
Missey, P.	5
Widow Mongeard	1
Morin, J.	14·4
Mugnier	1
Widow Noëllat	6
L'Héritier-Guyot (La Vigne Blanche)	4.75

The Arms of Clos de Vougeot

building, often referred to as a castle, which dominates the enclosure, started life as a monastery. The land, worked as a single vineyard, had been church property from 1089. Construction of the château started in the twelfth century and was not completed until 1551. It bears within every sign of being a botched job oft restored without great imagination. The story is that the original architect, a monk, committed one of the seven deadly sins, pride, by signing his plans before official approval by the Abbot. As a punishment the design was handed to a junior and very inferior colleague who ruined the original project, thereby killing the proud brother, who is said to have died of shame and a broken heart. The last monastic cellar master of the Clos, a lay brother appropriately named Dom Goblet, protested bitterly at his ejection after the Revolution on the sale of the property, but was astute enough to remove sufficient of his precious wine to keep him for the rest of his life. Being wise as well as unworldly, he never sold a drop of it.

The château has remained massively dignified but curiously undistinguished to this day, though considerable restoration and reconstruction has taken place through the centuries, probably the worst being in 1890.

The present owners of the château are the Chevaliers du Tastevin, the best known of all the Orders of Wine, founded in 1934. A final restoration and redecoration was needed after the last war, for the place was used as a billet by the Germans and later by the Allies, for prisoners of war. The massive stone-pillared *chai* in the courtyard is now their banquet hall, and an impressive job they have made of it, with a huge mural as a backcloth and their motto displayed with Gothic authority: 'Jamais en vain: Toujours en Vin!' A far cry from 'Cross and Plough.'

The great house is sparsely furnished and resembles a museum awaiting exhibits. Wine is no longer made here, but there are some huge presses of the fifteenth century in the barn-like *cuveries* which dwarf the visitor and put the business of producing wine in proper perspective.

The Chevaliers themselves, who dress as cardinals at the peak of their power, are a very astute body of men, all concerned with the promotion and consumption of the grape. They dine every other month about 500 strong, make new Knights of the Order, sing, orate and generally proclaim the glory of Burgundy. Their high feast day is the last Saturday in November, just before the sale of the vintage at the Hospice de Beaune, which itself is followed by the Paulée de Meursault, also a day of sales and banqueting.

These three days, known as *Les Trois Glorieuses*, are the peak of the year in Burgundy, the culmination of the season, for the *vendange* begins in early October and by mid-November each *vigneron* knows pretty well how he has fared. It takes giants, they say in Meursault, with the best of strong heads and stomachs, to stand up to these three celebrations, and this is not hard to credit.

Just as the mariners of Bordeaux used to dip their sails to salute the Grand Admiral of France at Beychevelle, so to this day troops who pass by Clos de Vougeot salute in its honour. This custom was established by a Colonel Bisson during the Revolution, who declared with perception that the vineyard contained the blood of France.

Rabelais described the wine as 'a delicious celestial god-given nectar', and in the days of the abbots the best of it, from the highest acres behind the monastery, was reserved for princes of the Church and State, a good deal finding its way to Rome, especially when favours were being sought. Certainly it has a royal quality and is traditionally the wine of kings.

Today Clos de Vougeot can be superb. 'Like silken velvet delicately scented with violets and truffles', say some sages, and 'Great as the vasty deep', but it is inconsistent, varying from owner to owner, and there are over seventy of them. However, to own even a quarter of an acre of this historic vineyard is so vital to every good vintner's reputation that no one treats the matter lightly: a status symbol is for something better than mere commercial gain.

Just outside the august walls there is a 5-acre field called '*La Vigne Blanche*' which makes a white wine, 'Clos Blanc de Vougeot', from Chardonnay grapes. These, it is now said, are not a Pinot blanc but a separate species. The wine resembles a Meursault and is not often seen in England, its standing being rather like that of White Haut Brion, which is to say that it is very

Illustration by the Author

One of the four fifteenth century wine presses in the cuverie *at Clos de Vougeot. These are now preserved as museum pieces but were in use for nearly five hundred years*

agreeable with cold salmon and, in my experience, with cheese and celery.

Flagey-Échezeaux

Behind the château of Vougeot, to the left as you face it, lie the vineyards of Flagey-Échezeaux, hyphenated in 1886, tucked away from the main road and particularly notable for Les Échezeaux and Les Grands Échezeaux.

Their fame in England is on the increase, largely through the acumen of Messrs Lebègue of London Bridge, but perhaps because of some difficulty in pronunciation they have not yet achieved the popular acclaim of their neighbours. Yet they are in the first rank, not perhaps as delicate as those of Vosne-Romanée, but of immense distinction, true Burgundy at its best. Grands Échezeaux is the more sought after, possibly, because there is less of it. This lack of publicity may account for the purity of the wine, for it has not been subject to variations at the hands of the less scrupulous merchants. It has certainly affected the price, which even today is less than that of either of the top people next door.

For anyone who wants to get to know how good a medium-cost Burgundy can be, here is what the consumer-protection people could well call a 'best buy'.

Vosne-Romanée

The small stone village of Vosne lies just off the main road and on the gentle slope above it are what many people consider the greatest wines in the world. Perforce the place is now called Vosne-Romanée. Since wine first became a matter for connoisseurs these vineyards have had unstinted praise. 'In Vosne there are no common wines', said Courtépée the historian in 1778 and this is still true. Even the first republicans recognized that this was a national asset, though they sold it without hesitation, but to a single purchaser. These priceless fields have had only nine different proprietors since the thirteenth century and continuity is one of the first essentials of wine-making.

The present major owners, the Domaine de la Romanée Conti, and the shipping firm of LeRoy are not people to play tricks

French Government Tourist Office

Vendanges on the Côte de Beaune. *The man is carrying a 'Hotte de Vendangeur', whose shape has varied very little through the centuries being made either of wood or leather. Some of the oldest are preserved in the Musée du Vin at Beaune and at Clos de Vougeot*

Vosne-Romanée

Têtes de Cuvées

	acres
Romanée Conti	4·5
La Romanée	2
La Tâche	15
Les Gaudrichots	3
Le Richebourg	12

Premières Cuvées

La Romanée-St Vivant	24
Les Beaux Monts	6·25
Aux Brulées	10
Les Malconsorts	15
Les Suchots	32·5
Aux Reignots	4·25
La Grande Rue	3·5
Aux Petits Monts	3

Flagey-Échezeaux

Têtes de Cuvées

	acres
Les Grands-Échezeaux	23
Les Échezeaux	106

Premières Cuvées

Les Beaux-Monts or Beaumonts	14
Champs-Traversins	9
Clos Saint-Denis	4·5
Les Cruots or Vignes-Blanches	8
Les Loachausses	10
En Orveau	25
Les Poullaillières	12·5
Les Quartiers de Nuits	6
Les Rouges-du-Bas	10
Les Treux	12·5

with so precious and expensive a heritage: their standards are inflexible and the product unique. 'In Vosne there are no common wines', and here the buyer can be sure of getting exactly what he expects – providing he can afford the price. La Tâche, for example, has a single owner, so there is no problem about finding the right Clos. La Tâche is La Tâche is La Tâche, as Gertrude Stein should have observed. Those who like research will be puzzled about the size of it. All the pre-war authorities, and this includes the *Atlas Vinicole,* which is a very precise volume, give it as 3½ to 4 acres. Today it is 15, according to M. de Henri Vilaine, the owner. The explanation is that some of Les Suchots has been included since 1925. The average yield is 350 barrels or 80,000 bottles.

Originally the Romanée land belonged to the Church, to the Priory of St Vivant, who sold it in 1625. In 1760 Madame de Pompadour, probably the shrewdest Royal mistress in history, made every effort to buy it for herself and would probably have succeeded had it not been for an even more astute competitor. He was the Prince de Conti, the very personal and private adviser-diplomat to Louis XV. It was he who gave the name Conti to what are probably the most valuable 4½ acres of vineyard in the world. He paid heavily for them, and when they changed hands in 1868 it was for £36,000, so their value has always been keenly appreciated. The average yield is eleven queues or 1,100 gallons, enough for only 550 cases.

A stone cross in the centre of these incomparable fields has been described as being 'at the very heart of wine'. It is true, for as one looks down the gentle slope to the village with Romanée St Vivant before you, to the left is Les Suchots, to the right La Tâche and Aux Malconsorts, whilst immediately behind are Romanée, Romanée Conti, and Richebourg.

There is no noticeable division between vineyard and vineyard in this rich carpet, and the new-comer might well wonder how it is that one wine could differ from another grown from apparently identical soil with an identical degree of care, yet within the strong family resemblance the features are individual and recognizable. 'This group unites all desirable qualities', says Camille Rodier, the great Chancellor of the Confrerie des Chevaliers de Tastevin, who of all men should know.

The Conti is generally considered the greatest, possibly on account of its scarcity: it has a lush, almost Oriental royalty about it and a superb balance which transforms any meal into a feast: indeed, it would be sinful to drink it as a mere accompaniment to a dish spiced with sauce by even the finest chef. It needs a plain roast with no high trimmings if its majesty is to be properly reverenced.

The same may be said of La Tâche, which I have known to surpass all its neighbours, though I confess I am thinking of a particular magnum of '47. La Romanée itself is the smallest of them all: there are only 2 acres of it. It is perhaps a shade softer and lighter, but is an aristocrat to the last drop.

Romanée St Vivant, the largest of the giants – 25 acres – dates as an entity from 1232, when the Duchess of Burgundy gave it to the Priory of St Vivant. It was the favourite wine of Louis XIV, Le Roi Soleil, who drank it as part of a cure for fistula and proclaimed that an illness which disclosed such a remedy was itself a present from Heaven. His physician, Fagon, who introduced him to the cure, has a street in Beaune named in his honour.

In 1870 when phylloxera ravaged the vineyards, most *vignerons* replaced their stock with hardy American roots on to which they have grafted, but in the Domaine they held on for over seventy years, and it was not until 1946 that the last of the famous 'pre-phylloxera' was replaced.

The burrowing louse who caused all the trouble is generally reckoned an American import, which is why American roots, now resistant to the brute, are used throughout France. Yet it first appeared disastrously in Burgandy in the middle of the fifteenth century and in 1553 Philippe de Berbis, the Vicar-General of Langres, ordered his clergy to put a curse in the name of God the Father on 'all such vermin and their posterity'.[1]

It seems to have worked the trick: perhaps the American invaders were beyond the range of this anathema, but at all events it kept France clear of trouble for over two centuries.

Le Richebourg, about 12 acres with its neighbour Les Variolles which is also sold as Richebourg, originally belonged to the Abbey of Citeaux and is the fifth star in this superb constellation.

[1] Camille Rodier in Le Clos de Vougeot.

The wine is elegant and has the quality of silk velvet: the 'fullest', it is said, of all the Romanées and perhaps more akin to the best of Clos de Vougeot. Like the rest of the quintuplicate, it has the additional virtue of being identifiable on demand: Richebourg has but one owner.

In all there are 370 acres of the best of Burgundy here, and in any other company the lesser growths would probably shine more brightly. Les Malconsorts, La Grande Rue, Aux Regnots, all of these are magnificently stylish fellows, right down to the second *cuvées* bearing the simple proud label 'Vosne-Romanée'. Anyone who is looking for an honest Burgundy of real quality need go no farther and the new-comer could not do better than to begin here.

Nuits St Georges

The pleasant old market town of Nuits straddles the River Muezin, which it spans with four stone bridges. It has around 3,000 inhabitants, all of them engaged in some way in the business of wine, and a modest hostelry, the Croix Blanche, named curiously after one of its least important fields on the wrong side of the main road which intersects it at right-angles to the river.

The words *'Negociant à Nuits St Georges'* on a wine label do not mean a great deal, except that the merchant keeps a registered office there, and carry no guarantee that the product comes from local vineyards, although the inference is intended. In the same way the town of Rheims, the centre of the Champagne business, is full of registered offices: not all of them are actual producers as their labels suggest. This also applies to Beaune.

True to form, the town added St Georges to its title in 1892 after its best-known vineyard, thereby inferring that every bottle entitled to the *Appellation* is of the quality of those notable 18½ acres which lie, in fact, farther from the town than any others. Les St Georges is right on the doorstep of Prémeaux, the next *commune*, but the division is not important, for both are entitled to the Nuits St Georges *Appellation*. Les St Georges is the centre section of a narrow three-mile-long slope all of which produces excellent wine.

Guy Gravett

Nuits St Georges. *After Beaune this pleasant little town is the centre of the wine business of Burgundy and the headquarters of many leading* négotiants

Nuits St Georges

Têtes de Cuvées

	acres
Le Saint-Georges	19
Les Boudots	16
Les Cailles	10
Les Porrets and Clos des Porrets	17·5
Les Pruliers	17·5
Les Vaucrains	15
Les Cras	7·5
Les Murgers	12·5
Les Thorey and Clos de Thorey	15

Premières Cuvées

Les Chaboeufs	7·5
Les Chaignots	14
Château Gris	6
Les Perrières and Clos des Perrières	7·5
Les Poulettes	6
Les Proces	5
Les Richemonnes	6
Les Roncières	5
Rue de Chaux	7·5

Prémeaux

Premières Cuvées

	acres
Le Clos de la Maréchale	24
Les Corvées	20
Les Corvées-Pagets	6
Les Didiers	7
Aux Forêts	12·5
Clos St. Marc	7·5
Clos des Argillières	12·5
Clos Arlot	19·5
Les Perdrix	8

Having said that, it must be faced that the quality varies very considerably; there are nine *têtes de cuvées* and nine *premières cuvées*, but the vast bulk of Nuits St Georges comes from the *Deuxièmes* and *Troisièmes*.

Even if the best of them do not approach the glories of Romanée Conti, they are fine, hearty specimens, fat and jovial and with the right stamina to stand up against any masterpiece of cooking in which the chef's prowess deserves first consideration. They are deep in colour, age slowly and keep well, being heavy in tannin. The names of the individual vineyards are important to note if you are looking for a wine of quality. Thus Les Vaucrains Nuits St Georges is an excellent label, whereas a simple 'Nuits St Georges' may be as workaday (and as good) as a bottle of Claret sold as St. Émilion.

Fairly recently a sparkling Burgundy from Nuits has appeared on the market. It is designed by the *negociants*, who have been experimenting since 1830 to compete in the Champagne market, and is almost universally frowned on or sneered at by gourmets. The open-minded should not be dismayed by this snobbery. As a drink it marches magnificently with roast pheasant, jugged hare or almost any game that is not fishy in flavour. What is more, it looks exciting whilst being no more intoxicating than any other wine. As a special item for a'teen- or deb-age party or dinner it can be highly commended as something out of the ordinary. It is also considerably cheaper than champagne.

Prémeaux, the next *commune*, really has no separate entity. Its 150 acres of vines are entitled to be classified as Nuits and are generally considered together, since they belong to the same strip of soil and taste much the same, if a trifle more delicately. Again the Burgundian watchword, '*Respectez les Crus*' should be observed; for example, 'Les Didiers St Georges', a wine of the same character but with an admired bouquet.

The Arms of Beaune

The Côtes de Beaune

The Hospice de Beaune

BEAUNE is even more a city of wine than Bordeaux, for its 14,000 inhabitants are almost entirely connected with the trade or religion, whereas the great port is a centre for all sorts of commerce.

It is as ancient in origin as history itself, starting as Belna of the Pagans, becoming Caesar's Bibracta, his headquarters in Burgundy, and finally Beaune after the arrival of the tribes. Cistercians, Carmelites, Benedictines, Carthusians, and Knights of Malta have all been vintners here. The Hospice de Beaune has owned vineyards and made wine to maintain its good works for 500 years. The vineyards which surround the town are among the first to be identified by name. The Clos de La Mousse was given to the Chapter of Nôtre Dame de Beaune in 1256. Today the Hospice de Beaune is the residuary legatee of all that remains of the clerical properties, a charitable trust which still endures. It maintains the showpiece of the city, the Hôtel Dieu built in 1443, which is still a hospital and old peoples' home conducted

French Government Tourist Office

The Hotel Dieu, the Hospice de Beaune. *Designed in 1443 by the Flemish architect Jacques Viscrere for Nicolas Rollin, the alms house with its multi-coloured tiles, though characteristically Flemish, is considered one of the masterpieces of France. Wine sales are held here every year and the hospital is still in full use as an old people's home. Every section of it, including the kitchens, is of interest to visitors*

by nuns who serenely ignore the constant traffic of the world's tourists come to admire this curious architectural masterpiece. Nicolas de Rolin and his wife Guignonne de Salins built it as an alms house. He was the Chancellor of Burgundy in his day, a relentless tax-gatherer for Philippe le Bel, and it was said of him by Louis XI that 'having rendered so many poor and homeless he could well afford to make his peace with the Almighty by providing for them'. Successive legacies in the way of vineyards, if they have not made the Hospice rich, have at least enabled the good sisters to maintain it just as the founders intended. A new hospital, however, is on the way and soon the Hospice itself will be nothing but a showpiece. Fifty old people live here permanently now, sixty children are cared for and educated, and the poor of all the neighbouring parishes are eligible for help and nursing.

It is here in the main hall against a background of tapestries and vats that the great wine sale takes place each year on the third Sunday in November, the second of 'Les Trois Glorieuses'. It is the most important date in the Burgundian calendar, for it is the day on which each *vigneron* whose land is owned by the Hospice exposes his new vintage to buyers for the first time and the world's wine merchants pass judgement with the acid truth of money. It also sets a standard of prices for all Burgundies, although only wines from the mixed bag of 125 acres of the property are offered for sale, and those in such an early stage of their life that many of them are, as they say, 'still working', and can be heard doing so if you listen carefully.

It is an occasion for much ritual: bidding for each lot is limited in time by that forerunner of clocks, a marked candle, although the ceremony, in fact, only dates from 1899.

The wines here are sold in cask and many of them are bought for prestige reasons by *restaurateurs* who consider the advertisement worth the price. The proceeds go to the upkeep of the Hospice. The wiser *negociants* make other arrangements, realizing that young wines need darkness and silence to reach sound maturity. The best of Beaune is not sold at this stage at all, but is bottled on or near the original estate. Still the ritual, the feasting, and the fun continues, and the pattern of price for the year is set.

The wines of the Hospice, of which the best and dearest is

Desmond O'Neill

The Gateway to Beaune. *The town is the ideal centre for tourists and apart from its great architectural interest has three first class restaurants, specializing in the dishes of the area*

probably the *cuvée* of Nicolas Rolin, are not necessarily all Beaune, but can come from all around the Côte. The name Hospice de Beaune on a bottle means that the vineyard is their property and is the gift of benefactors through the centuries.

After the best has been sold at the great auction the lesser liquid is distilled and thereby transformed into a Marc de Bourgogne, or *eau-de vie*.

This rather raw spirit seems to me to have all the charm of Irish cooking brandy, but it is much prized throughout France, though placed below the Marc de Bordeaux, which can, when prepared by a good château, Mouton Rothschild for example, have a quality which is unmistakable.

Beaune is a walled city, full of winding streets, a jumble of periods, and the ground beneath is honeycombed with enormous cellars whose capacity is forever increasing. The cellars of Lebègue-Bichot seem like a city in themselves. The Street of the Wine Merchants is the most picturesque, but the centrepiece is the Hospice, with its cobbled courtyard, its long sweeping medieval Flemish roof of multi-coloured tiles, and its imperturbable peace.

There are several notable hostelries: the Poste and the Marché are rosetted in Michelin, who omits the Hôtel de la Cloche altogether, which will seem curious to those who know the town.

The average is extremely high; probably the best food and wine in Burgundy is to be found here. The specialities are crayfish in cream, Potée Bourguignonne, smoked hams and Coq au Vin – dishes designed to show the magic of Meursault, Chambolle-Musigny, Corton, and Chambertin.

Aloxe-Corton

The Côtes de Beaune itself starts north of the town with Aloxe-Corton, the most illustrious name in the whole diadem. Little Aloxe added its hyphen in 1862. Clos du Roi and Corton itself are its finest red products. Both are slow to mature and not so long-lived as the best of the Côtes de Nuits. They are lighter, perhaps more debonair than the northerners, but beautifully balanced princes as befits vineyards once owned by the Emperor Charlemagne, the first Christian master of Europe. It

Aloxe-Corton

Têtes de Cuvées

	acres
Le Corton	28
Le Clos du Roi	26
En Charlemagne	42·5
Les Chaumes	6
Les Renardes	37·5
Premières Cuvées	
Les Bressandes	42·5
Les Chaumes de la Voirosse	
Les Perrières	20
Les Fietrus	
Les Grèves	
Les Meix-Lallamant	
La Vigne-au-Saint	

Note: Where the acreage is not defined it is extremely small, usually 2 acres or less.

Beaune

Têtes de Cuvées

	acres
Les Fèves	11
Les Grèves (inc. de l'Enfant Jesus)	79·5
Les Marconnets	25·5
Les Bressandes	46
Les Clos des Mouches	62
Les Cras	12·5
Les Champimonts	41·5
Les Clos de la Mousse	8·5
Some Premières Cuvées	
A l'Écu	8
Sur-les-Grèves	11·5
Clos du Roi	35
Les Cent-Vignes	58
Aux Coucherias	56·5
Chaume-Gaufriot	48
Montée-Rouge	41·5
Les Chilénes	42·5
Les Theurons	19

Guy Gravett

St Romain, Hautes Côtes de Beaune. *Better known for the making of wine casks. St Romain is a decorative hillside village surrounded by lesser vineyards which still have the right to the appellation 'Côtes de Beaune'. La Ruchot, le Plain de Lugny, Sous le Marsin and Les Parolles are among them*

was he who established the traditions of clerical ownership by giving his fields to the Abbot of Sanlieu. He also gave his name to one of the best of white wines, Corton-Charlemagne, a golden drink which is peer to the Montrachets.

The Clos du Roi dates from 1477, when Charles the Fearless, that reckless autocrat, established it by filling in marshy land. He was the last of the Dukes of Burgundy, which was just as well, and the land passed from him to his arch-enemy Louis XI of France, thus acquiring the Royal accolade.

Le Corton and Corton-Charlemagne are in the hands of expert *vignerons* and can be bought without fear of disappointment. The terrain is not for idlers, for the slopes are steeper than any on the entire Côte and the soil must be constantly protected against erosion by water from the wooded hills above and replaced if the winter torrents succeed in sweeping it away. The wines have the liveliest ruby colour in all Burgundy and mature at about seven years.

The *crus* here take Corton as a first name, the vineyard itself following, as in Corton les Bressandes. Eumenius, the Roman rhetorician of Autun, who visited these parts in 311, thought highly of the vineyards, which he regarded even then as ancient. So did Voltaire, who boasted, privately, that he kept Corton for himself and served Beaujolais to friends.

Savigny-les-Beaune, farther up the hillside from Aloxe, is its lesser sister so far as production goes. The village, cut into two by the stream Rhion, is a mildly picturesque collection of hillside houses, and the best of the wine comes from those upland slopes, which have a favourable southern aspect and are protected by the woods above them. Les Vergelesses, Les Marconnets, and Les Jarrons, are the cream of them, all fairly large yielders. Their savour is said to suggest a mirabelle plum and they have a light fresh bouquet of raspberry, but the wines are overshadowed by those of Beaune, though they are true Burgundians and their names are sufficiently unknown to free them from unscrupulous attention.

Beaune

Here the vines run in a continuous belt west of the city and form the largest acreage of first growths in all the land,

Volnay	
Têtes de Cuvées	acres
Les Caillerets	36
Les Champans	28
Les Premiets	16
Les Angles	9
Some Premières Cuvées	
En Chevret	15
Glos des Ducs	6
Clos des Chênes	41
Village de Volnay	32·5
Robardelle	10·5
Les Lurets	21
Grands-Champs	17·5
Brouillards	17

Pommard	
Têtes de Cuvées	acres
Les Épenots	26
Les Rugiens-Bas	15
Le Clos Blanc	11
Some Premières Cuvées	
La Platière	14·5
Les Pézerolles	16
Les Petits-Épenots	51
Les Rugiens-Hauts	19
Clos de la Commaraine	10
Les Jarollières	8
Village de Pommard	65

producing an average of 86,200 gallons a year of *Têtes de Cuvées.*

They can be drunk when comparatively young, since they have a shorter fermentation period than most, but never so young as the French would have you believe. Allow at least three years. They are very clean and smooth and make excellent companions for almost any meat course, being solid enough to stand up to competition in the matter of flavours on the palate and to complement the best.

Historic echoes abound. Les Grèves, for example, was the property of the Carmelites for several centuries. They named one corner of the clos *La Vigne de L'Enfant Jésus* after the arms of the city of Beaune, which display the Virgin with the child on her arm and in her hand a vine with grapes.

For me this is the perfect Burgundy, and my reason for saying this is not (as it so often is with such a statement) sentimental. It is because I have never encountered any bottle of this gentle velvet delight which was short of perfection in its class, and the price is within reason. If I said that it had for me the quality of the Gregorian 23rd psalm bass and treble, then sentiment does arise: but how else can the translation be made? This corner of the Grèves vineyard now belongs to Bouchard Père et Fils, one of the best of the shippers.

Since Beaune is the biggest of the Côtes from the point of output it follows that it is also the best known. 'A bottle of Beaune' is thought of as a safe and modest request in a restaurant or at a wineshop. If that is the most that is sought, then all is well, for the wine is plentiful and, like St Émilion, its counterpart in Claret, it is generally reliable. But it should be remembered that there are 2,500 acres of vines, by no means all of them planted with Pinots, and of them only 165 produce *Premier Crus*. Beaune is worth asking for in detail if its true quality is to be enjoyed: the *Cuvée* should always be specified or you will be landed with a respectable mediocrity.

Les Grèves is among the best, as are Les Fèves and Les Marconnets. Clos des Mouches, despite its unfortunate name, is a fine full-bodied fellow. A very good white wine is made from Chardonnay grapes in the same clos.

Probably the safest of the lesser labels, a reliable companion for any meal, is 'Côte de Beaune-Villages', an *Appellation Contrôlée*. Here you must put faith in your merchant and trust that he has bought wisely in cask and bottled with skill. The wine so sold is a careful amalgam of the produce of many growers and a good specimen should have all the general characteristics of Burgundy and yet be a cut above a simple Beaune with no other specification. It is reasonably priced and is as good an introduction to the greater ranks as any beginner could wish, whilst remaining a respectable entity in its own right.

Pommard

Unhyphenated Pommard is a prosperous photogenic village, full of charm as befits so celebrated and popular a name. It is intersected by the River Dheune and by a little canal, built to ease the swift winter flow of water from the hills above. It is a place of ripples, little humped bridges, cobbles, and leaning branches. All around are the vines separated by low stone walls. The main road from Beaune to Autun passes its toe, but misses the centre. The name derives from Pomona, the Roman goddess of fruits and gardens, whose temple once stood here. The eminent Courtépée

Guy Gravett

Château La Rôche-Pot, *in the Hautes Côtes de Beaune is an example of the type of mansion which is common in the Bordeaux district but is extremely rare in Burgundy. Most vinyards were monastically owned and few great houses survived the Revolution. Château La Rôche Pot which is moated, dates from the fifteenth century and has the curved conical turrets which are also found in the fortifications of Chablis*

1

2

3

Photos: Desmond O'Neill

(1) The Great Hall of the Hospice de Beaune during the annual wine sale on the third Sunday in November. The room is hung with tapestries, the one shown includes the Virgin and Child with vine which is the crest of Beaune

(2) The Auctioneer taking a bid at the Sale. The candle on the right is used to limit the duration of the bidding. The last bid taken before it goes out is successful

(3) A wine 'Dégustation', one of the many set up in the streets of Beaune during the week of 'Les Trois Glorieuses', the great wine sales of Clos-de-Vougeot, Hospice de Beaune and Meursault. It marks the peak of the year locally and is attended by buyers from all over the world

mentions it as being known long before the Domesday Book was compiled and Victor Hugo, whose tastes were hearty, wrote in its praise.

The fame of Pommard, until the *Appellation Contrôlée* came into force, was also the cause of its fall from informed popularity. Of all wines it has been the most subject to sharp practice, partly because the name sits easily on the English tongue and partly because the area was a centre of Protestantism and the Huguenot refugees fleeing from persecution in the seventeenth century gossiped nostalgically of the lost glories of their homeland.

The wine is long-lived and improves with age. It is full-blooded and firm, a man's drink with an attractive fruity bouquet, and there is a great deal of it, 1,570 acres in all. Here, possibly more than anywhere in Burgundy, the watchword *'Respectez les Crus'* is important. The town name should always precede the *Cuvée*, as for example: 'Pommard-Les Épenots' or 'Pommard-Les Rugiens-Bas'. These two vineyards are classed as outstanding.

Volnay

South of Pommard by a mile is the village of Volnay, set in rolling country, some of it high enough to command views right across the whole plain.

The wine has a long-standing reputation for gaiety, perhaps because it is lighter in colour than its neighbours, with a fresh flowery bouquet which makes it appear remarkably good-tempered. *'On ne peut être gai sans boire de Volnay'* is the local boast.

The best of Volnay and the largest vineyard, 36 acres, is indisputably Les Caillerets: a connoisseur's wine, which is not to say it cannot be appreciated by ordinary mortals. Maurice Healy recalls a bottle of 1889 as being the finest he ever drank. It was over thirty years old then and surpassed even La Tâche 1904 and Richebourg 1923, the companions in his great triumvirate of perfection. They are, curiously, all Burgundies, though his main devotion was to Claret.

The vineyards are of the same Roman lineage and were particular favourites of the conquerors, who left many traces of their occupation in the way of terra-cotta amphora. During the early days of the Roman ban on the planting of vines it was the custom

Guy Gravett

Château Pommard, Côtes de Beaune, *is the property of La Flanche Ainé, one of the two fine mansions in the village, the other being the Château de la Commaraine. The vines are longer lived than those of Volnay: they are firm, vigorous and with great body*

for the local *vignerons* to effect a nominal sale of their land to any occupying citizen or soldier of status, whose right it was to grow wine for his own use, and many of the fields hereabouts date from this sensible evasion of autocracy.

In later centuries a wine which must have been a sort of rosé was made here, called '*vin de paille*', the wine of straw often mentioned in early French literature. The name derives from the practice of laying out the grapes on straw matting so that they could dry out and catch the last of the autumn sun before pressing. It is still made at the Arbois, in the Jura. It was abandoned here in the seventeenth century, when the qualities of the Pinot became more widely appreciated.

On balance there is rather more good Volnay to be had than Pommard and this is because the outstanding vineyards are individually larger.

The wines mature early and the best of them live to a considerable age, though all Burgundies need to be watched very carefully after twenty years and there is no recompense for the unexpected death of a favourite.

Auxey-Duresses, the next village, is not of major interest for its wines, most of which are shipped in bulk if they go overseas and appear under a general label. Duresses is not unexpectedly the best vineyard of what used to be Auxey without the hyphen. The wine is very like a Volnay and can attain a rich mellowness with age, along with a bouquet. It is a slow maturer.

The village itself is on rocky ground on the bank of the River Meursault and with its neighbour Monthelie, high above it, makes up the last of the Côte de Beaune proper, for south of it on the right bank of the river, which here makes a steep ravine, the subdivision of the Côte de Meursault starts. The Monthelie wines are like those of Auxey, very little of them reaching the overseas market except as 'Côte de Beaune', by which time they have been astutely blended into a reasonably priced drink with no outstanding personality.

Meursault

This little town of less than 2,000 inhabitants is one of the most attractive miniatures in Burgundy. The name is reputed to derive from 'Muris Saltus' ('mouse jump'), a relic of Roman days, the inference being that it was but the leap of a mouse between the red vineyards and the white. History has touched it at every epoch and left its mark at each episode, from the Stone Age to the Liberation on September 6th, 1944, by the 1st French Armoured Division.

It seems to have been a perpetual point of assembly for more northerly battles and Louis XI demolished its fortress and ramparts in an attempt to prevent further trouble.

Despite this, and the destruction by fire of one of the châteaux

Guy Gravett

Volnay. *Many of the vineyards here belonged to the Knights of Malta and the wine has always had a high reputation in France. Louis XI in 1447 reserved the entire vintage for his own use at the Château of Plessy-les-Tours. The most delicate of the burgundies, its bouquet is said to resemble a raspberry*

in 1594, Meursault continued its story of blood and upheaval. It was notorious for its anti-religious masquerades in the Revolution. At the break-up of the big properties a wily citizen called d'Arnay-le-Duc managed to buy up the entire acreage of vines which he sold off very profitably in small packets, many of which have now been amalgamated.

Through all this the making of wine has continued without break since the Romans, who left a fine stone portico in the

Place du Merger as one of their marks. Here, too, there is a Hospice, though of lesser fame than at Beaune.

Meursault as a name means only white wine to most people, but in fact there are four vineyards north of the town which produce reds almost the equal of its neighbour Volnay. Indeed, the Santenots-de-Milieu is known as Volnay-Santenots and is among the best of the Volnays and is really only a Meursault by a vagary of topography. The rest of the reds are sold as Côtes de Beaune.

But the fragrant graceful glory of Meursault is white and has few peers and possibly only one superior in all the hierarchy of Burgundy. The Compte de Moucheron of the Château de Meursault, who has holdings in Les Perrières and Les Charmes, which are the leading *cuvées*, in a noteworthy pamphlet in English, says: 'The situation of these vineyards severely examined reveals always that they are among the best fitted to supply a wine of remarkable delicacy and bouquet. Owing to this double wisdom the vintages of the Château de Meursault have an unvarying goodness which is hardly found elsewhere.'

It is largely true, and certainly the château, built on the site of the one destroyed in the seventeenth century, has the finest cellars in the district.

They are twelfth-century monastic work, enormous, and as sound today as ever. This is one of the few houses in all Burgundy where there is genuine château bottling, the corks being branded and the wines, from whichever vignoble they come, being made in the *chai*.

De Moucheron has other holdings in Burgundy, notably at Chambertin and Montrachet, but his main cellars are at Meursault. He is also a leading shipper.

The soil hereabouts is stiff and has the reputation of being the most difficult to work in all the Côte. This is the origin of La Paulèe, derived like our own 'pause' from the Greek *paula*, the midday rest taken by the *vignerons*. Since 1922 it has also been identified with the Harvest Home Feast in Meursault now held at the Caveau St Vincent, which is the third of *Les Trois Glorieuses*.

The Hôtel du Chevreuil, the best of the inns in Meursault, is now conducted by Pierre Thevenot, a relative of the *vignerons*

Meursault

Têtes de Cuvées	acres
Clos des Perrières with Les Perrières	42·5
Some Premières Cuvées	
Les Charmes	39
Les Genevrières	42·5
Santenots (if red sold as Volnay)	20
Sous-Blagny	5·5
Le Pièce-sous-le-Bois	28
Second Growth	
La Goutte d'Or	14

who have holdings in Goutte d'Or, the best of the second growths. The entailed speciality of the house, the *terrine chaud de Madame Dauzier*, is a fine delicacy mainly composed of highly spiced rabbit, cooked, I suspect, with Vermouth.

Despite the very large number of small holders, Meursault seems less subject to fraud or variation than most wines. This is probably because it is one of the easiest to identify on the palate. The outstanding *cuvées* are in the master class and the lesser growths, without exception, make for most civilized drinking.

My own stay in Meursault was an idyllic episode which maybe casts a nostalgic spell, but I have never tasted an indifferent bottle of that pale golden magic. This includes, specifically, Goutte d'Or, one of the second growths, which can be found in England, though it is popular locally. If you ask for a good Meursault in the village, this is what is usually offered.

Puligny and Chassagne

These two villages or *communes* both tag the magic word Montrachet to their names. The 19 acres of Le Montrachet itself lie across the border of each and both are anxious to be associated with such glory, for this is the greatest of the white Burgundies beyond a peradventure, and for my money the finest white wine in the world.

Guy Gravett

The Clos de la Pucelle *at Pouligny Montrachet, a vineyard of 16½ acres which produces one of the Premières Cuvées. The village of Pouligny is in the background. The stone entrance is typical of the marking of the* finages *south of Beaune*

Pouligny-Montrachet

Tête de Cuvée

	acres
Montrachet (part in Chassagne)	10

Premières Cuvées

Le Chevalier-Montrachet	15·5
Le Bâtard-Montrachet	24
Bienvenue-Bâtard-Montrachet	6
Les Combettes	17
Champ-Canet	11·5
Pucelles	16·5
Les Chalumeaux	17·5

Chassagne-Montrachet

White Wines:

Tête de Cuvée

Montrachet (part in Puligny)	9

Premières cuvées

	acres
Le Bâtard-Montrachet (part in Puligny)	32·5
Les Ruchottes	7·5
Morgeot	9·75
Cailleret	15
Criots-Bâtard-Montrachet	4

Red Wines:

Têtes de Cuvées

Le Clos Saint-Jean	36
Clos de la Boudriotte	5
Les Boudriottes	40
La Maltroie	23
Champgain	71·5
Les Brussanes, Le Grand Clos, and Le Petit Clos	45

As with Clos de Vougeot, the ownership of even half an acre of these wines is a status symbol in the world of wine, and the purchase price often outweighs the profit to be made from them. Montrachet, by the way, is pronounced Monrachet and can be translated as 'The Bald Hill', a reference to the treeless slope on which the vines grow. There are sixteen owners in all and it can almost be said that each grape receives individual and expert attention. Alexander Dumas declared that the wine should be drunk on the knees, bareheaded, and many of the devout would agree with him.

'Divine Montrachet!' it has been called, and for many of us it is the world's masterpiece as a white wine. In her incomparable presence Yquem becomes a dumb blonde, relying on curves and diamonds, and the most expensive of the Germans an over-scented Valkyrie. She is Millament played by Edith Evans: Fonteyn outbidding Nureyev.

At the price which each bottle commands, the invitation to fraud is considerable, and of all wines this is the most important to buy estate-bottled.

The three great Montrachets in order of merit and cost are the Montrachet itself, Chevalier-Montrachet, and Bâtard-Montrachet. To describe these riches in words is not for mortals, but the limpid authority, the flawlessly clean touch on the palate, the bouquet of almond and the effortless vigour of them are outstanding.

In colour they are very pale with a touch of green and tend to deepen to gold in age. The authorized strength is 12 per cent, the highest on the Côte.

They require very careful handling and should always be stored in the coldest part of any cellar. For this reason, though estate-bottled, the various proprietors do not keep them locally, for the ground has many underground springs and deep cellaring is impossible.

The Chevalier, the Montrachet, and the Bâtard lie one above the other on the same slope. Next door is what used to be called, and still is on some maps, Les Demoiselles. I do not understand what sort of prudery made the French change the name, for this is not normally one of their characteristics, but the vineyard is now called Le Cailleret, which means clotted or congealed – a gross libel on beautiful wine.

The Montrachet itself and the Bâtard lie half in the Chassagne *finage*. The latter's exclusive wines are headed by Les Ruchottes, closely followed by Cailleret and Morgeot. All of these have a dry flowing charm of their own. Despite this they lack the fame of the Pulignys and are therefore mercifully less expensive. They are a living proof that he who selects his wine by price alone is either a man in a hurry or a foolish fellow.

Much the same could be said of the red Chassagnes, which are not nearly so well known as they deserve. They follow the general character of the best of the Nuits, but are a trifle lighter, very soft and well tempered. The growers, who have a biased view, maintain that they can be drunk young, but Les Boudriottes, the largest of them, keeps well and should be allowed at least five years. The Clos Saint Jean, established in 1390, is noteworthy.

Santenay, the final *commune* on the Côte de Beaune, has only one wine of interest, the red Les Graviens, and most of the large output is sold under an all-purpose label.

Région de Mercurey

These vineyards are often called the Côte Chalonnaise, though they are some distance from the town. Mercurey is the best of them and indeed the only name of any standing in England. The *finage* takes its name from the temple of Mercury, which once stood there. The site is marked only by a sail-less windmill, but he is an appropriate deity for Burgundy, being, according to one school, the son of Bacchus and Prosperina and cupbearer to the Gods until he was sacked as an incorrigible thief in favour of Ganymede.

He is the patron of orators, merchants, shepherds, and thieves, and among his large progeny was Pan himself.

With such eminent patronage it is remarkable that Mercurey is not a greater wine. It has been described as a poor relation of Volnay and no doubt a good deal of it has been palmed off on the innocent under the nobler label. It is a lighter affair altogether, but with an agreeable fruity bouquet, and is made from the Pinot, though the territory of the Gamay and the Petit Gamay begins here.

Rully, Givry, and Montagny are the other *commune* names recognized by the *Appellation Contrôlée* and both red and white wines are made. The fact must be faced that these are all lesser brethren, 'sound dinner wines', as the old fashioned wine merchants used to say, light and amiable, extremely agreeable in a carafe with sandwiches or an omelette at a bistro. The best of them, the Clos St. Pierre at Givry, is given the status of second growth of Beaune, which is a kindly rating. It may be that my personal opinions are coloured by the fact that the countryside hereabouts is remarkably dull and that Chalons has nothing to arrest the inquiring tourist except the Hôtel Royal, where the trout and the sauce that goes with the frogs legs are so good that the local wines can take a comfortable second place.

Photograph: The Author

Bacchus *called Dionysus by the Greeks was the youthful, beautiful but effeminate Roman God of Wine. Noisy and riotous he was a favourite subject for XVIII century Franco-Italian sculptors. This statue, the souvenir of an English Milord's Grand Tour, is in the gardens of Layer Marney Towers in Essex.*

The Arms of Mâcon

The Mâconnais

MÂCON, capital city of Saône et Loire, sits beside the last of the great white-wine fields, the land of the Pouillys. The ancient town is a landmark for travellers, for here the south begins. Here shade starts to become important and roofs overhang walls; the pace of life slows for the sun.

It was a centre before the Romans came. They fortified it, called it Castrum Matisconensis and established their vineyards. Attila the Hun destroyed it: the Burgundii settled there. Charlemagne incorporated the area in his conquests, and the Royal Saint, Louis IX, acquired it in 1238 by purchase, for although a crusader he was in principle a man of peace.

The medieval cathedral was largely destroyed in the Revolution and not a great deal remains in the town to show its history.

Cluny, the great religious centre a few miles west, which fared much better from the point of architectural survival, is really the parent of the present vineyards. The monks of the Abbey of La Firte made the first of them and they are still there.

There are two heroes of Mâcon. The more eminent is the

poet-politician Lamartine, who was born there and kept a shooting lodge at Milly, near by, though he lived at the Château Monceau, where he grew vines. His most important lyric work is *La Vigne et La Maison*, written in 1857, which might be described as Wordsworth with wine. He married, with great happiness, an English girl called Maria Birch, and though at one point he enjoyed an enormous success in both his vocations he died like so many true poets in poverty.

The second hero is the courageous *vigneron* called Claude Brosse, who was the first man with sufficient enterprise and strength to make the journey from Mâcon to Paris in 1600, where the wine was unknown, with a couple of barrels, here called Foudres, of his own product.

It took him a month, for his oxen were not to be hurried and the road was infested with footpads. Having arrived at Versailles, he dutifully attended mass in the presence of Louis XV himself. His great height caused him to appear to be standing when he was in fact upon his knees, and for this apparent irreverence he was hailed before the King, who had noted what he took to be blasphemy. His Majesty was delighted at this discovery of a giant in a Court which loved dwarfs, and Brosse did not hesitate to explain his errand in Paris and to demonstrate his wares. He was an instant success.

The King having praised them, the Court followed in extolling the virtues of Mâcon, and its fame was established.

It was certainly a red wine which the brave Brosse took to Paris, but the aristocrats of the area are the white Pouillys.

There are five communes with the right to the *appellation* Pouilly-Fuissé, and the best of it comes from around the tiny hamlet of Fuissé itself.

Like Chablis, it is very pale, with a slight greenish tinge, and can be drunk young, though it can be comparatively long-lived. 'Twenty years do not exhaust its strength and on the contrary adorn it with new grace', says M. Mommessin, an official authority and an eminent shipper. All the same, it is risky to let so good a thing overripen, and at five years most of the Pouillys are at their best.

They are clean, refreshing wines, wholly admirable with fish, chicken or cheese, with the fragrance of young nuts dipped in

Guy Gravett

The Mill at Moulin à Vent. *The sail-less windmill which is a landmark, is preserved as an historic monument. It stands at the heart of Moulin à Vent, the best of the Beaujolais wines. It is here that the miller is reported to have discovered that hot soapy water would kill the phylloxera louse which was devastating the wines of France*

melon. The best grape is the white Chardonnay, but for the *ordinaires* the Aligote is used.

The demand for Pouilly is enormous and world wide, and production, or at least labels, have a tendency to match such a state of affairs. It is wisest, therefore, to be specific in buying and to choose something with a more detailed name than the simple *Appellation Contrôlée.*

The Château de Pouilly, Le Peloux, and Aux Clos are among the best of the Pouilly simple. Of the Fuissés the Château de Fuissé leads the field, along with Les Clos and Les Vignes Blanches.

The whole area is dominated by a remarkable rock formation, the Roché-de-Solutré, which looks very like Gibraltar from the south-east. All but the last few feet can be climbed by motorists and the panorama from the little stone rostrum at the top, especially on a day of cloud and sun, is dramatic. The Solutré wines are a shade less virile than their neighbours, which tend to be heady when young, but have the same general character. Above Solutré is the *commune* of Vergisson and at the far end of the Mâconnais is Chaintre, 1,000 acres in all, which have the right to the Pouilly-Fuissé *Appellation Contrôlée.*

A little red wine is made, but it is no more than a *vin du pays.*

The Arms of Beaujeu

Beaujolais

Just south of Pouilly the last, and in some ways the best known, of the vineyards of Burgundy, the Beaujolais, begins. This fame has greatly increased since the war, for there is a great deal of Beaujolais and it is the cheapest of the good red wines. It is also the most abused of all labels: I would not like to guess what proportion of so-called Beaujolais comes from Algeria, but it must be considerable. Here the Gamay comes into its own, for it gives of its best in granite soil.

This is the area of co-operatives, and nearly every one of the dozens of villages and hamlets in the district has its own tasting stall or '*dégustation*', gay with canvas awning, at its centre. You may be offered it free or for as much as ninepence a glass. Unlike other tastings, those held in cellars, this is a complete pleasure, for Beaujolais is one of the few wines which can truly be drunk young, whereas the important Burgundies at a year should never get beyond the collar stud and have to be expelled. Moreover, ordinary mortals do not have the experience needed to judge an immature wine whose taste bears little relation to its possible future. A motorist who is not afraid for his tyres can wander here happily for days and get delightfully lost in the process, for the hillsides curve and the narrow roads twist with them. They are fully entitled to the words 'Route Pittoresque', beloved of map-makers when they mean that the surface is probably abominable but the landscape is worth it.

The best known of them is the Moulin-à-Vent, a hillside vineyard dominated by another windmill without sails. It is here that the celebrated *vigneron* lived who made the great discovery about the cure for phylloxera in the plague of the 1870s which destroyed three-quarters of the vineyards of France.

In flinging away a bucket of boiling soapy water, on his wife's instruction, he spattered those vines nearest his kitchen door and was delighted to find that he had killed the pestilent louse who was causing all the trouble.

The centre of the Beaujolais district was originally the little town of Beaujeu, a few miles south-west of Fleurie, once the seat of the Sires of Beaujeu, the overlords of the district. It still keeps its pleasant motto: *'A tout venant – beaujeu'*, and indeed the whole sunny area offers a welcome in smiles and wine. For a modest pocket there was never a wine better named, for even if you call it Bowjolly it suggests warmth and amiability, its main characteristics. It is a wine for drinking deep and young, 'between the cellar and the top of the stairs' and is short-lived. Five years is the normal span.

The best of the *finages* after Moulin-à-Vent are Fleurie, Morgon, Chénas, Brouilly, and Juliénas. For my money Fleurie is the most acceptable, for it has a quality of velvet and raisins and varies very little. But they are all, within their sound workaday limits, most excellent drinking, stout-hearted as Brosse himself, and civil companions for any school of cookery, whether high or low.

I have commended wandering idly, perhaps *'Dégustation crawling'* is the phrase, among these villages, and I can think of no pleasanter pastime, but the wise gourmet will go due east, to the wrong side of the tracks to discover the village of Thoissey and visit the Chapon Fin, a restaurant of two-rosette eminence set among trees, conducted impeccably by M. Blanc. It specializes in duck, *crêpes*, and local wine, and far surpasses its namesake in

Bordeaux which had once the same standing. For those moving rapidly south along the route national, Les Compagnons de Jehu at Pontanevaux, though ominously appropriately named, is worth noting.

This is the area of the Beaujolais pot, a three-quarter size bottle which is now finding its way to England. Reasonably large enough for two, it is a very convenient measure. Most of the wines so bottled are the product of co-operatives and are the better for it.

At Chazay-d'Azengnes the Beaujolais ends abruptly, and within a few kilos the horrid suburban outposts of Lyons spread their red-brick tentacles. My advice is to make a detour to Tain-l'Hermitage or to turn the chariot sharply about and to move gently northwards again, towards the vineyards of Chablis. A recap is always a stimulating precaution and it is good to meet old friends.

The Best of Beaujolais

Vineyards:	*Communes:*
Moulin-à-Vent	Fleurie
Les Carquelins	Morgon
Mortperay	Brouilly
Les Chants-de-Cour	Juliénas
Les Burdelines	

Guy Gravett

A *Cuverie* in Beaujolais. *One of the many to be found in every village in this country, run on co-operative lines. The grapes are brought in directly from each small holder's vineyard, pressed communally and are said to be ready for drinking by the following spring. They may be sampled by the roadside at stalls for 'dégustation' set up in each village*

Some Books on French Wine

MAURICE HEALY, Stay me with Flagons

LOUIS JACQUELIN and RENE POULAIN, The Wines and Vineyards of France

P. MORTON SHAND, A Book of French Wines

ANDRÉ SIMON, The Noble Grapes and the Great Wines of France

DENIS MORRIS, The French Vineyards

ALEC WAUGH, In Praise of Wine

RAYMOND POSTGATE, The Plain Man's Guide to Wine

ALEXIS LICHINE, Wines of France

C. W. BERRY, In Search of Wine

H. WARNER ALLEN, The Contemplation of Wine

H. WARNER ALLEN, Through the Wine Glass

T. E. CARLING, Wine Aristocracy

ANDRÉ SIMON, A Wine Primer

ALLAN SICHEL, The Penguin Book of Wines

* * *

LOUIS CRIZET, Les Vins de France

LOUIS CRIZET, Le Vin

Le Vin de France dans L'Histoire

GEORGES BOUCHARD, Le Vin Bourgogne

PIERRE POUPON and PIERRE FORGEOT, A Book of Burgundy

Les Vins de Bourgogne

Baccarat glasses. *The bowl on the extreme left was designed especially for drinking Romanée Conti, whereas that on the right is the most favoured shape for Burgundies generally*

Some Burgundy Vintages

1962 Good and prolific, especially for Chablis and most whites.

1961 Poor generally, but better for Mâconnais and Beaujolais.

1960 Average for Chablis and other whites. Poor for Beaujolais. Bad for reds.

1959 Great year all round. Best for whites.

1958 Only fair for all wines. Good for Meursault.

1957 Good for Chablis and most other whites. Fair for reds.

1956 Mediocre for Chablis owing to frost. Average for whites and reds.

1955 Very good all round. Red wines of this year are now reaching full maturity.

1954 Mediocre for Chablis owing to frost. Average for Beaujolais. Mediocre for whites and reds.

1953 Very good for Chablis. Excellent and promising for whites. Good and full-bodied for reds.

1952 Good for Chablis and all whites. Very good and full-bodied for reds. Now getting rare.

1951 Poor for Chablis. Mediocre for whites. Average to thin for reds.

1950 Fair for Chablis. Good for Beaujolais. Fair for whites. Good for reds.

1949 Great for all wines, particularly reds.

1948 Very good for Chablis, great bouquet and vintage character. Average for Beaujolais. Average for whites. Very good and delicate for reds.

1947 Good for Chablis. Great and rich for all others, fine bouquet and very supple.

1946 Very good indeed for Chablis. Very good for all reds and whites. Fine bouquet with supple wines.

1945 Very good for reds and whites, both full-bodied. Frost killed Chablis, which would be too old now anyhow.

1944 Mediocre and thin for reds and whites.

1943 Good all round. Vigorous reds with body.

1942 Good all round. Fine bouquet.

1941 Mediocre for reds. Fair for whites.

1940 Mediocre for reds. No whites at all.

1939 Mediocre for reds. Average for whites.

1938 Average for reds. Good and vigorous for whites.

1937 Good and full-bodied reds. Bad for whites.

1936 Bad and thin reds, poor whites.

1935 Bad for all wines.

1934 Very good for reds, if still alive. Good for whites.

1934 Very good for reds, if still alive. Good for whites.

Very few Burgundies are alive now beyond this date. For red wines the following older vintages may be noted:

1929
1928
1926
1923
1915

A tastevin *used for displaying and examining the colour of wine. The fluted bowl reflects from every angle*

SERVING BURGUNDY

All wines should be stored on their side and only taken into the dining-room during the last two days of their life. Burgundies should be uncorked not more than an hour before drinking, except when very old, when a few minutes is ample. They should be allowed to become 'chambré', that is to reach room temperature, or in England a trifle above. In emergency the wine can be decanted into a warmed carafe, or a hot cupboard has great virtues. A cheap wine can be improved considerably by judicious warmth, but this should never be applied rapidly.

A basket cradle is a useful way of serving wine bottled by your own merchant, but it should never be used with a domaine-bottled wine, which once upright should stay that way.

White wine can be cooled by a short spell in a refrigerator, which is more efficacious than an ice bucket.

The necks of bottles should be wiped very carefully after uncorking.

The thinnest glass is the best for any wine. It should never be more than two-thirds full to allow it to breathe. A red wine if served too chilly will show increased virtue if the glass is warmed in the hand before drinking.

The shape called 'tulip' is probably the most practical, but if you are feeling rich Messrs Baccarat make some superb glass particularly designed with the masters like La Romanée in view.

White wines, the Montrachets for example, often improve considerably if allowed to lie in the glass for a minute or two before drinking. The second glass of any wine is generally better than the first, partly for this reason and partly because the first glass will clean your palate.

The French consider that Beaujolais can be served slightly cooled, but this really is only applicable in very warm weather, when it is drunk principally as a thirst quencher.

A magnum of good Burgundy is generally superior to two bottles of the same vintage, and vastly ahead of four half-bottles. A magnum develops more slowly than a bottle or a half-bottle, and is the most likely to live long.

A Glossary of Wine Terms in Burgundy

Cave *Caveau*	A cellar, also a wine shop.
Chai	A barn-like chamber at ground level where wine is made, containing vats and presses.
Climat	A vineyard. The word here derives from Climate, the exposure, soil, etc., of the area.
Clos	Strictly, a walled vineyard. In general a defined area of vines.
Corsé (of wine)	Full, vigorous.
Cru	A classification by quality *Cru hors ligne:* an outstanding wine.
Cuvé	A vat.
Cuvée	An individual wine. When used as '*Tête de Cuvée*' the best wine. Also, vatting. The contents of a vat.
Feuillette	A half-cask: 144 bottles.
Finage	A parish or area. A *commune.*
Foudre	A hogshead barrel: a Mâconnais term. Also a large vat for wine blending.
Hectare	2·47 acres of land or 100 French ares.
Ouvrée	A tenth part of an acre.
Pétillant	Very slightly effervescent. A quality in a rosé, but something to be wary of in a red.
Pièce	A hogshead or half a *Queue*, containing 226 litres, the equivalent of 288 bottles. The measure varies regionally.
Queue	100 gallons. 456 litres or 600 bottles. The standard Burgundian measure of yield. From the Roman *Culeus.*
Tastevin	A small silver bowl fluted to reflect light, used for tasting wine and assessing quality.
Vigneron	A worker in the vineyards, but often signifying the owner.
Vignoble	Vineyard.

ACKNOWLEDGEMENTS

I am extremely grateful to the French Government Tourist Board, Mr E. L. de Rouet of Brown, Gore and Welch, Mr Guy Prince of Lebègue, Mr Adrian Ball of Fleet Street, Harveys of Bristol, W. & A. Gilbey, M. George Bouchard of Bouchard Ainé, Mr John Wheeler of Lay and Wheeler, Mr Peter Waugh, Mr Guy Gravett and Mr John Hortin, all of whom have given me great assistance with all that is best in this book.

A final toast to the vendange. *The scene is a cellar in Beaujolais during a visit by English buye*
It can be described as that of a government public relations officer salesman and adviser

Guy Gravett

e host, centre left, is a 'Conseiller de Commerce', a position of high official standing in France. no counterpart in Britain. The author is on the extreme left

The Vintage. *A tapestry of the XVth century now in the Musée Ochier at Cluny, the great vineyards in Burgundy*

medieval religious centre from which the Cistercians migrated to create some of the best